NEW KENT AND HANOVER COUNTY [VIRGINIA] ROAD ORDERS

1706-1743

Virginia Genealogical Society
Richmond, Virginia

Published With Permission from the

Virginia Transportation Research Council
(A Cooperative Organization Sponsored Jointly by the Virginia
Department of Transportation and
the University of Virginia)

HERITAGE BOOKS
2008

HERITAGE BOOKS

AN IMPRINT OF HERITAGE BOOKS, INC.

Books, CDs, and more—Worldwide

For our listing of thousands of titles see our website
at
www.HeritageBooks.com

Published 2008 by
HERITAGE BOOKS, INC.
Publishing Division
100 Railroad Avenue #104
Westminster, Maryland 21157

International Standard Book Number: 978-0-7884-3658-1

NEW KENT COUNTY AND HANOVER COUNTY ROAD ORDERS 1706-1743

Transcribed from the Vestry Book of St. Paul's Parish

by

Ann Brush Miller

Senior Research Scientist

Virginia Transportation Research Council
(A Cooperative Organization Sponsored Jointly by the Virginia
Department of Transportation and
the University of Virginia)

Charlottesville, Virginia

March 2004
VTRC 04-R17

DISCLAIMER

The contents of this report reflect the views of the author, who is responsible for the facts and the accuracy of the data presented herein. The contents do not necessarily reflect the official views or policies of the Virginia Department of Transportation, the Commonwealth Transportation Board, or the Federal Highway Administration. This report does not constitute a standard, specification, or regulation.

HISTORIC ROADS OF VIRGINIA

Louisa County Road Orders, 1742-1748, by Nathaniel Mason Pawlett. 57 pages, indexed, map.

Goochland County Road Orders, 1728-1744, by Nathaniel Mason Pawlett. 120 pages, indexed, map.

Albemarle County Road Orders, 1744-1748, by Nathaniel Mason Pawlett. 57 pages, indexed, map.

The Route of the Three Notch'd Road, by Nathaniel Mason Pawlett and Howard Newlon. 26 pages, illustrated, 2 maps.

An Index to Roads in the Albemarle County Surveyor's Books, 1744-1853, by Nathaniel Mason Pawlett. 10 pages, map.

A Brief History of the Staunton and James River Turnpike, by Douglas Young. 22 pages, illustrated, map.

Albemarle County Road Orders, 1783-1816, by Nathaniel Mason Pawlett. 421 pages, indexed.

A Brief History of Roads in Virginia, 1607-1840, by Nathaniel Mason Pawlett. 41 pages.

A Guide to the Preparation of County Road Histories, by Nathaniel Mason Pawlett. 26 pages, 2 maps.

Early Road Location: Key to Discovering Historic Resources? by Nathaniel Mason Pawlett and K. Edward Lay. 47 pages, illustrated, 3 maps.

Albemarle County Roads, 1725-1816, by Nathaniel Mason Pawlett. 98 pages, illustrated, 8 maps.

"Backsights," A Bibliography, by Nathaniel Mason Pawlett. 29 pages, revised edition.

Orange County Road Orders, 1734-1749, by Ann Brush Miller. 323 pages, indexed, map.

Spotsylvania County Road Orders, 1722-1734, by Nathaniel Mason Pawlett. 159 pages, indexed.

Brunswick County Road Orders, 1732-1749, by Nathaniel Mason Pawlett. 81 pages, indexed.

Orange County Road Orders, 1750-1800, by Ann Brush Miller. 394 pages, indexed, map.

Lunenburg County Road Orders, 1746-1764, by Nathaniel Mason Pawlett and Tyler Jefferson Boyd. 394 pages, indexed.

Culpeper County Road Orders, 1763-1764, by Ann Brush Miller. 22 pages, indexed, map.

Augusta County Road Orders 1745-1769, by Nathaniel Mason Pawlett, Ann Brush Miller, Kenneth Madison Clark and Thomas Llewellyn Samuel, Jr. 284 pages, indexed, map.

Amelia County Road Orders 1735-1753, by Nathaniel Mason Pawlett, Ann Brush Miller, and Kenneth Madison Clark. 157 pages, indexed, map.

Fairfax County Road Orders 1749-1800, by Beth Mitchell. 326 pages, indexed, map.

Requests for information and regarding availability of these publications should be directed to:

Historic Roads of Virginia
Virginia Transportation Research Council
530 Edgemont Road
Charlottesville, VA 22903

www.virginiadot.org/vtrc/history/roadordr.html

INTRODUCTION

by

Ann Brush Miller
Virginia Transportation Research Council

The roads are under the government of the county courts, subject to be controuled by the general court. They order new roads to be opened whenever they think them necessary. The inhabitants of the county are by them laid off into precincts, to each of which they allot a convenient portion of the public roads to be kept in repair. Such bridges as may be built without the assistance of artificers, they are to be built. If the stream be such as to require a bridge of regular workmanship, the court employs workmen to build it, at the expense of the whole county. If it be too great for the county, application is made to the general assembly, who authorize individuals to build it, and to take a fixed toll from all passengers, or give sanction to such other proposition as to them appears reasonable.

Thomas Jefferson
Notes on the State of Virginia, 1781

The establishment and maintenance of public roads were among the most important functions of the county court during the colonial period in Virginia. Each road was opened and maintained by an Overseer of the Highways appointed by the Gentlemen Justices yearly. He was usually assigned all the "Labouring Male Titheables" living on or near the road for this purpose. These individuals then furnished all their own tools, wagons, and teams and were required to labour for six days each year on the roads.

Major projects, such as bridges over rivers, demanding considerable expenditure were executed by commissioners appointed by the court to select the site and to contract with workmen for the construction. Where bridges connected two counties, a commission was appointed by each and they cooperated in executing the work.

Virginia's first road laws (in 1632 and 1657 [*Hening* v. I, pp. 199, 436]) put the basic control of county roads under the control of the county courts. Under the expanded 1661 road legislation (*Hening* v. 2, p. 103), the vestries of the Established (Anglican) church were noted as potential adjuncts to the function of the county court in transportation-related matters. At the request of the surveyor (overseer) of the road, the vestry could order the tithables along the route to work on the road:

... the vestryes of every parish are upon the desires of the surveyors hereby enjoyned and impowered to order the parishioners every one according to the number of tithables he hath in his family, to send men upon the dayes by the surveighors appointed to helpe

them in clearing the wayes, and making or reparing the bridges according to the intent and purpose of this act. . . .

Thus, although the majority of Virginia's colonial road and transportation-related records can be found in the order books of the county courts, some road records may be found within vestry records. Such involvement by the vestry was the case in St. Paul's Parish, Hanover County, until well into the 18th century. In the case of Hanover County, for which the early court records have been destroyed, vestry records are the only remaining records regarding the early roads in the region.

The vestry records arguably do not contain every transportation-related order issued by the county court during the period, but they are concerned with the allotment of districts and laboring tithables for the various overseers of the roads. Apparently the vestry's involvement was largely ceded to the county court at some point in the second quarter of the 18th century: the road-related orders noted in the vestry book virtually cease after the late 1730s, with only one order (for 1743) recorded after that date. Several land processioning orders and tobacco viewing orders that make reference to roads can also be found in the vestry book, and these have been included in a separate appendix.

A peculiarity of the original records is reflected by the fact that each entry can be cited by several page numbers. Because of damage to portions of the vestry book, the original pagination does not survive on all pages. Prior to the original volume being photostated during the first part of the 20th century, the pages were renumbered. A typed note inserted into the photocopy documents the situation:

> *This book contains Photostat prints of the first part of the St. Paul's Parish Vestry Minute Book in the Episcopal Theological Seminary Library near Alexandria, Virginia.*
> *It was necessary to bind the prints into two books instead of one owing to the fact that the photostat paper is very thick and that reproductions are made only on one side. The original pagination having been lost in part, new page numbers were added with a pencil before the process of reproduction was begun. Both page numbers are to be seen on many of the pages. They are easily distinguished from each other.*
> *The first part of the original is very dilapidated.*

In addition, a transcription of the vestry book, edited by Dr. Churchill Gibson Chamberlayne, was published by the Virginia State Library in 1940. In the current volume, all three page numbers (original, 20th century renumbering, and Chamberlayne transcription) are given for full reference.

At its creation in 1704, St. Paul's Parish included the western portion of New Kent County, which became Hanover County in 1721. Hanover County in its original boundaries extended westward to the Blue Ridge, and included modern Hanover County, Louisa County (created from Hanover in 1742) and the northern third of what is now Albemarle County (part of the western portion of Louisa until 1762, then added to Albemarle County).

For over two decades, St. Paul's Parish included, at least nominally, the entirety of old Hanover County, running westward toward the Blue Ridge Mountains. During this period, settlement extended into what is now Louisa County and began to extend into eastern Albemarle County.

In 1727, St. Paul's Parish was divided. The region east of the South Anna River and Stonehorse Creek remained St. Paul's, whereas the part of the county to the west of those watercourses became St. Martin's Parish.

New Kent County and Hanover County Road Orders 1706-1743 marks a departure from the previous volumes of road orders published by the Virginia Transportation Research Council, as it contains road orders that are not among the records of the county court. This volume covers the surviving Hanover County transportation records for the first half of the 18th century and includes the earliest surviving transportation-related records for a significant parent county of central Virginia.

This publication marks the twenty-second entry in the *Historic Roads of Virginia* series, first initiated by the Virginia Transportation Research Council (then the Virginia Highway & Transportation Research Council) in 1973.

A NOTE ON THE METHODS, EDITING, AND DATING SYSTEM

by

Nathaniel Mason Pawlett
(Faculty Research Historian, Virginia Transportation Research Council, 1973-1995)

The road and bridge orders of an early Virginia county are the primary source of information for the study of its roads. When extracted, indexed, and published by the Virginia Transportation Research Council, they greatly facilitate this. All of the early county court order books are in manuscripts, sometimes so damaged and faded as to be almost indecipherable. Usually rendered in the rather ornate script of the time, the phonetic spellings of this period often serve to complicate matters further for the researcher and recorder.

With these road orders available in an indexed and cross-indexed published form, it will be possible to produce chronological chains of road orders illustrating the development of many of the early roads of a vast area from the threshold of settlement through much of the eighteenth century. Immediate corroboration for these chains of road orders will usually be provided by other evidence such as deeds, plats, and the Confederate Engineers maps. Often, in fact, the principal roads will be found to survive in place under their early names.

With regard to the general editorial principles of the project, it has been our perception over the years as the road orders of Louisa, Hanover, Goochland, Albemarle, and other counties have been examined and recorded that road orders themselves are really a variety of "notes," often cryptic, incomplete, or based on assumptions concerning the level of knowledge of the reader. As such, any further abstracting or compression of them would tend to produce "notes" taken from "notes," making them even less comprehensible. The tendency, therefore, has been in the direction of restraint in editing, leaving any conclusions with regard to meaning up to the reader or researcher using these publications. In pursuing this course, we have attempted to present the reader with a typescript text that is as near a type facsimile of the manuscript itself as we can come.

Our objective is to produce a text that conveys as near the precise form of the original as we can, reproducing all the peculiarities of the eighteenth-century orthography. Although some compromises have had to be made because of the modern keyboard, this was really not that difficult a task. Most of their symbols can be accommodated by modern typography, and most abbreviations are fairly clear as to meaning.

Punctuations may appear misleading at times, with unnecessary commas or commas placed where periods should be located; appropriate terminal punctuation is often missing or else takes the form of a symbol such as a long dash, etc. The original capitalization has been retained insofar as it was possible to determine from the original manuscript whether capitals were intended. No capitals have been inserted in place of those originally omitted. The original spelling and syntax have been retained throughout, even including the obvious errors in various places, such as repetitions of words and simple clerical errors. Ampersands have been retained throughout to include such forms as "&c" for "etc." Superscript letters have also been retained where used in y^e, y^t, s^d. The thorn symbol (y), pronounced as "th," has been retained in the aforesaid "y^e," pronounced "the," and "y^t" (that). The tailed "p" (resembling a capital "p" with the tail extended into a loop) has also been retained. This symbol has no counterpart in modern typography; given the limitations of the modern keyboard, we have rendered it as a capital "p" (P). This should be taken to mean either "per" (by), "pre," or "pro" (and sometimes "par" as in "Pish" for parish) as the context of the order may demand. For damaged and missing portions of the manuscripts, we have used square brackets to denote the [blank], [torn], or [illegible] portions. Because of the large number of ancient forms of spelling, grammar, and syntax, it was deemed impracticable to insert the form *[sic]* after each one to indicate a literal rendering. Therefore, the reader must assume that apparent errors are merely the result of our literal transcription of the road orders, barring the introduction of typographical errors, of course. If, in any case, this appears to present insuperable problems, resort should be made to the original records.

As to dating, most historians and genealogists who have worked with early Virginian records will be aware of the English dating system in use down to 1752. Although there was an eleven-day difference from our calendar in the day of the month, the principal difference lay in the fact that the beginning of the year was dated from March 25 rather than January 1, as was the case from 1752 onward to the present. Thus January, February, and March (to the 25th) were the last three months in a given year, and the new year came in only on March 25.

Early Virginian records usually follow this practice, though in some cases, dates during these three months will be shown in the form 1732/3, showing both the English date and that in use on the Continent, where the year began January 1. For researchers using material with dates in the English style, it is important to remember that under this system (for instance) a man might die in January 1734 yet convey property or serve in public office in June 1734 since, under this system, June came *before* January in a given year.

THE ACT TO ESTABLISH ST. PAUL'S PARISH

Note: The bill to divide St. Peter's Parish, which would establish the western portion of the parish into the new St. Paul's Parish, was passed by the General Assembly of Virginia in May 1704. The act is recorded in *Hening* v. 3, p. 225 by title only. A complete copy is in the British Record Office (C. O. 5/1384), from which the following section is taken. This section gives the bounds of the old and new parishes and also mentions several existing roads.

An Act for dividing S.ᵗ Peters parish in New Kent County

Whereas Sundry and divers Inconveniencys attend the Inhabitants of S.ᵗ Peters Parish in New Kent County by reason of the largeness of the Extent of the said parish Be it therefore Enacted by the Govern.ʳ Council and Burgesses of this present generall assembly and the authority thereof And it is hereby Enacted that on and after the first day of June next the said parish of S.ᵗ Peters be divided into two distinct parishes and that the Division of the said two parishes be from the mouth of Maccadecum creek, So up the said Creek to M.ʳ John Lewis his mill, thence down the Queens high road to the Rowling road that goeth from Edward Moors to George Turners so along the said road including the said Moor in yᵉ upper parish, thence along the said road to the plantation of John Baughan Senior who is to be in the upper parish thence upon a line between the plantations of Nicholas Lawson and John Sandidge the said Lawson to be in the Lower parish and Sandidg in the upper and so upon a streight line to Chickahominy Swamp including Edward Clarks in the upper parish, and that the lower part of the said parish shall remaine and hereafter be called and knowne by the name of S.ᵗ Peters parish, and that the upper part of the said parish shall hereafter be called and known by the name of S.ᵗ pauls parish.

NEW KENT COUNTY AND HANOVER COUNTY ROAD ORDERS 1706-1743

from the Vestry Book of St. Paul's Parish

Note: *Each entry is cited by several different page numbers. The first page number refers to the original vestry book pagination. The vestry book was renumbered in the 20th century, prior to photocopying, and "new pagination" refers to this later system. Pagination with the notation "Chamberlayne" refers to the transcription of the vestry book edited by Dr. Churchill Gibson Chamberlayne and published by the Virginia State Library in 1940.*

[page torn] January[?], 1705/6[?], Old Style, no original pagination visible [new pagination p. 447; Chamberlayne pp. 1-2]

Pursuant to an Order of Court, Appointing M,ʳ John [torn] of the high ways dated July 29.ᵗʰ 1695. the s.ᵈ Mr John White [torn] himself to the vestry of S,ᵗ Pauls Psh in the manner & form fo[torn] The bounds of the precincts which M,ʳ John White, was appoin[torn] of as followeth.

Beginning at the mouth of Elder Swamp running up it to the he[torn] branch of Mattedicun, call'd little Creek, down that to the Fork, wh[torn] Lancaster formerly dwelt, than up that Creek P, Polegreens Quarter, [torn] of Beaver dam Swamp, then down that, & the main Swamp, to the [torn] Elder Swamp, where it began.

[page torn] January[?], 1705/6[?], Old Style, no original pagination visible [new pagination p. 447; Chamberlayne p. 2]

Ordered, that all contain'd within the above limits, give their du[torn] in Clearing the high ways, According to the former Order of Court.

]page torn] January[?], 1705/6[?], Old Style, no original pagination visible [new pagination p. 447; Chamberlayne p. 2]

An acc,ᵗ of Tithables this day Ordered Edw,ᵈ Harris Surveyo [torn]s, Pursuant to an Ord,ʳ Court, dated 7br. 28ᵗʰ 1704; on t[torn] [torn]topottomys Creek, viz, Geo; Sheperson, Jnᵒ Tap, Jnᵒ [torn]eadly, James Jennings, John Elderkin, with all [torn] of the said Creek, including M,ʳ Thomas Poind[torn].

[page torn; date not visible], Old Style, no original pagination visible [new pagination p. 446; Chamberlayne p. 3]

[torn]nt to an ord,ʳ Court dated march 30,ᵗʰ 1690, Appointing [torn]nderson Surveyor of the high Ways, now Applying himself [torn]try of S,ᵗ Pauls parish, whose Limits are as followeth, viz; [torn] at Tottopottomoy's Creek, including that bridge, and so up [torn]y's Swamp, Ordered, that Mahixon Gang, middle Quarter [torn]y's Quarter, Widdow Youell, Doctor Brabant, Ely Davis, [torn]hn Ray, give yʳ due attendance in Clearing the said [torn]ays, bounded as aforesaid, in obedience to the above [torn] Court.

January 1, 1706/7, O.S, p. 14 [new pagination p. 13; Chamberlayne p. 17]
In Obedience, to an order of new Kent County Court, bearing Date the 28.th of 8br, 1706 wherein it was Ordered that John Johnston to be an Overseer, of a new road from Cacy's, Old field, along an old path down to Stony Swamp, and so down Another path, that goes to M,^r Craffords Mill; but this Vestry finding that this road is Altogether inconvenient to those Inhabitants, therefore they have not Ordered Any Assistance therein

April 2, 1707, O. S., p. 15 [new pagination p. 14; Chamberlayne p. 18]
Pursuant to an Ord.^r of Court bearing date January 28.th 1706 Appointing William Harriss to be Surveyor of a new Road in the Forks, he now Applying himself to this Vestry, It's Ordered that all the Tithables, of the north Side of the South River in the Forks and William Terrell on the South Side of the River (or Allotted Tithables for to Assist him, in Clearing and making a Road According to the Contents of the S,^d Order of Court

October 1, 1707, O. S., p. 16 [new pagination p. 17; Chamberlayne p. 22]
Persuant to an order of Court dated July y^e. 28th 1707 Appointing M^r. David Anderson, and Samuel Waddy to Clear Paumounkey river on the South side thereof, from the pipeing Tree, to Harding's Landing, formerly Youels, they applying themselves to the vestry for assistance with Instruments, or materials for to comply with the Said Order; This Vestry has thought, that the parish is not able to Comply with that Order

January 1, 1707/8, O.S., p. 17 [new pagination p. 18; Chamberlayne pp. 23-24]
In Obedience to an Ord,^r of new Kent County Court, bearing Date 9ber. ye 28.th 1707. Appointing Abraham Cook Surveyor of a Bridle Road, from Maj,^r Meriwethers Mill, to the three runs of Chickohommany Swamp, he applying himself to this Vestry for Assistance; Its therefore Ordered that John Kimbrow Jun,^r John Venable, Alexander Cock, Henry Bowe, Thomas Peak, William Williams Humphrey Parrish Jeremiah Parker, Stephen Sentre, John Wootton, Rob,^t Cook William Wetherford, & Tho,^s Wetherford, forthwith give their attendance in making a Road

January 1, 1707, O.S., p. 17 [new pagination p. 18; Chamberlayne p. 24]
In Obedience to an Order of New Kent County court bearing date Jan.^{ry} 28.th 1706/7 Appointing Christopher Clark Surveyor of a new horse Bridge which Should be made Over Bever Dam Swamp, he applying himself to this Vestry for assistance; Its therefore order'd that Alexander M,^ckenny, Tho,^s Caisey, William Hogg Thomas Bowls, Edward Clark, Tho,^s Bailey, Tho,^s Johnson Isaac Winston, and Nathaniel Hodkison, give their attendance in making the Said Bridge.

February 14, 1707/8, O.S., p. 17 [new pagination p. 19; Chamberlayne p. 25]
Ordered that the Following Tithables shall be added to and belong to the Precincts of M,^r John White (viz) Mark Anthony's, John Hall's, Elizabeth Burnett's, Edward Bullock's Frances Esther's & Elizabeth Evins, (which lately belong'd to the precincts of Capt Robert Anderson) also M,^r Rowland Horsleys, John Lawson's & Wm Freeman's which lately belong'd to the precincts of Joseph Baughon

March 14, 1708, O.S., p. 21 [new pagination p. 26; Chamberlayne p. 32-33]
In Obedience to an Ord,[r] of this County Court, dated Jan,[ry] 8,[th] 1708 we do appoint John Perkins Sen,[r] his Tithables, John Perkins Jun[r] his Tithables, Edward Chambers his Tithables, John Tyler, Joseph Gentry Richard Corley, Jun,[r] John Tinsley, and one Tithable of M,[r] Henry Chiles's to assist Nicholas Gentry (who is Appointed Overseer by the Aforesaid Ord,[r] of Court) in Clearing and keeping in Repair the road mention'd in the Said Order.

April 26,1709, O.S., p. 21 [new pagination p. 26; Chamberlayne p. 33]
Upon the Complaint of Nich,[s] Gentry, that his assistance is not able to make his road passable; Its Ordered, that M,[r] Henry Chiles, James Nuckols and Abraham Cook each of them send four Tithables out of their Precincts, to assist the Said Nich,[o] Gentry two days to make Bridges over Crump's Creek, and the Deep Swamp.

August 8, 1709, O.S., p. 21 [new pagination p. 27; Chamberlayne p. 34]
Pursuant to an Order of new Kent County Court held March 28,[th] 1709 Ordered that all the Male Tithables living on this Side Paumonkey River and on the north Side of the main Road, from Esquire Lewis's Mill, to this Church, including John Guntins & Col,[o] Bassett's Quarter, for the uppermost, assist M,[r] John Mask, in Clearing and keeping in Repair the Roads mention'd in the Said Order, and also that they keep the Said Main Road in Repair from the Said Mill, to the Old Schoolhouse near Samuel Waddy's Plantation

April 11, 1710, O.S., p. 24 [new pagination p. 32; Chamberlayne p. 40]
In Obedience to an Order of new Kent Court, dated 28th Feb,[ry] 1709/10 Its ordered that Henry Mills, Joseph Poors, Joseph Brown Henry Farmur, Col,[o] Dukes Quarter, Roger Smith, Charles Rhodes, William Howlet, Samuel Rennolds, John Byas, Rob,[t] Walker John Kimbrow Jun,[r] John Harris, Rennold Allen, W,[m] Hatfield and Daniel Dishman, with all their Male Tithables, are to Assist John Glenn to clear the road According to the said order of Court

October 8, 1712, O.S., p. 31 [new pagination p. 46; Chamberlayne p. 57]
In Obedience to an Order of New Kent County Court dated the 11,[th] of 9br, 1712, its Ordered, that Issack Winston have Jn[o] Pirant Nath,[l] Hodgkinson, Joseph Hambleton, Maj,[r] Meriwether's Lower Quarter, Tho,[s] East, and Tho,[s] Basset, & their Male Tithables to Assist him in Clearing a Road from M,[r] John White's Mill, to half Sink

October 8, 1712, O.S., p. 31 [new pagination p. 46; Chamberlayne p. 57]
In Obedience to the same Order its ordered that Alex,[r] M,[c]kensie have Cap,[t] Roger Thomson's Md: Clough's M,[r] Peter Tickle's Edw;[d] Clark Xph.r Clark, Tho,[s] Bowle's; W,[m] Hogg & Tho,[s] Kersey to Assist him in Clearing a Road, from M,[r] Jn[o] Whites Mill to Polegreens Old Field

September 26, 1713, O. S., p. 33 [new pagination p. 50; Chamberlayne p. 62]
Persuant to an order of Court dated July y[e]. 9th 1713 Appointing M[r]. David Anderson, & Samuel Waddy to Clear Paumonkey River on the South side thereof, from the Pipeing tree to Harding's Landing they Applying themselves to the Vestry for Assistance, with Instruments, or Materials to comply with the S,[d] Order, This Vestry is of Opinion that the parish is not able to Comply with that Charge

October 15, 1715, O. S., p. 36 [new pagination p. 56; Chamberlayne p. 71]
Whereas M[r]. David Anderson appeared this day with an Order of Court to Clear Paumonkey River on the South Side from the Pipeing Tree to Harding's Landing, & for this Vestry to Assist him with men & materials to perform the same. – This Vestry is of opinion as formerly they have been, viz, that this parish is not Able to Comply w,[th] that Charge

January 2, 1715/16, O.S., p. 36 [new pagination p. 57; Chamberlayne p. 73]
By a Petition of M[r] Alex:[r] Cock, its Ordered that Henry Bowe Tho,[s] Dick, Rich,[d] Allen, and John Hudson, assist the Said Cock in Clearing a Road from Possom Point into the main road, Leading down the Country, Below Bassets runs & that when the said road is Clear'd, they are to return to their former precincts

September 22, 1716, O.S., p. 37 [new pagination p. 59; Chamberlayne p. 75]
In Obedience to an Order of new Kent County Court, dated y[e] 8,[th] day of march 1715, its Ordered that Jeremiah Parker, have Frances Clark: Jn[o] English, Jn[o] Venable, Jn[o], Corley, Sam,[l] Sperring, W,[m] Webb, Paul Bunch's Quart,[r] Tho,[s] Wetherford, Gilbert Gibson, W,[m] Thacker, Stephen Raglin, & John Hart, with all their Male Tithables to assist him in Clearing a road from Stony run downward to half sink road

September 22, 1716, O.S., p. 37 [new pagination p. 59; Chamberlayne p. 75]
In Obedience to the same Order its Ordered that all the tithables from Golden mine Creek, to Stony run, with M,[r] Geo: Dabney's Quarter, and Thomas Harris, do assist Sam,[l] Gentry in Clearing a road, from Stone Horse Creek, to Stony run

April 23, 1717, O.S., p. 38 [new pagination p. 61; Chamberlayne pp. 77-78]
In Obedience to an Order of new Kent Court dated 9br, y[e]. 8.th 1716 Ordering Roger Thomson Gent, to Survey a road, & Clear a Road from Poles green's Old Field, to Hardings Store house, its Ordered, that the Said M,[r] Thomsons Male Tithables at his home house, and Cha: Bostick, assist in the Clearing, & maintaining the S,[d] Road

November 19, 1717, O.S., p. 39 [new pagination p. 62; Chamberlayne p. 80]
Order'd, that Rob,[t] Mills assist John Glenn in maintaining the road he is Surveyor of

November 19, 1717, O.S. p. 39 [new pagination p. 63; Chamberlayne p. 80]
Orderd, that John Ray be added to M,[r] Henry Chiles precinct, to assist him in maintaining the Road he is Surveyor of

October 10, 1719, O.S., p. 42 [new pagination p. 68; Chamberlayne p. 86]
In obedience to an order of Court dated y,^{e} 12.th of March 1718 Ordering Tho:^{s} Anderson to clear a Bridle Road from Jno Anderson's to Alex,^{r} Cocks, its Ordered that M,^{r} Jno Macon's Male Tithables Cicilia Anderson's ditto, Gilbert Gibson, Geo: Thomas, Tho,^{s} Sattawhite David Thomson, Henry Bow, & John Hambleton, assist the said Anderson in Clearing and maintaining the Said road

October 10, 1719, O.S., p. 42 [new pagination p. 68; Chamberlayne p. 86]
In Obedience to an Order of Court dated ye 13,th of August 1719 Appointing William Talley Surveyor of the road from M,^{r} W,^{m} Flemming's Mill to Mahixen path, its Ordered that the Tithables that belonged to the said road, assist the said Talley in keeping the road in good order

October 10, 1719, O.S., p. 42 [new pagination p. 69; Chamberlayne p. 88]
At a Court held August 13.th 1719, Wherein M,^{r} David Meriwether was Ordered to Clear a Road from Maj,^{r} Nich,^{o} Meriwether's to the new Church--its Ordered, that John Lewis Jun,^{r} Jno Saunders, George Philips, Rob,^{t} Netherland and Thomas Glass, with all their Male Tithables assist, Mr David Meriwether in Clearing and maintaining the said road

October 10, 1719, O.S., p. 42 [new pagination p. 69; Chamberlayne p. 88]
In Obedience to an Order of Court of ye same date, wherein Mr William Flemming was made Surveyor of the road, from Tottopottomoys Creek to Samuel Waddy's, its Ordered that ye usual Tithables assist the said Flemming in maintaining the said road

July 3, 1720, O.S., p. 43 [new pagination p. 70; Chamberlayne p. 89]
In Obedience to an order of Court dated may 20th 1720 Ordering Thomas Stanley to Clear a Road, from Ceder Creek to the road that goes to new market Mill, its orderd, that the said Stanley have all the Tithables between Newfound river, & Ceder Creek, untill he Comes to the Gang, Belonging to M,^{r} John Glenn

October 29, 1720, O.S., p. 44 [new pagination p. 72; Chamberlayne p. 92]
Ordered that M,^{r} David Meriwether have James Tate's & Jno Hill's Male Tithables, and Edward Penix, to assist him in Clearing and maintaining ye road he is Overseer of.

October 29, 1720, O.S., p. 44 [new pagination p. 72; Chamberlayne p. 92]
Order'd, that Jere: Parker have all the Male Tithables below Stony run between Chickahominy Swamp, and the branch of Machump's Creek, by Cornelius Tinsleys including M,^{r} Cha: Hudson, and from thence to Megirts path, to Tottopottomoy's Creek and from thence to the mouth of Stony run

October 29, 1720, O.S., p. 44 [new pagination p. 73; Chamberlayne pp. 92-93]
In Obedience to an order of Court dated ye 22.^{d} of may 1709; its order'd that M,^{r} John Anderson, have M,^{rs} Mary Anderson's male Tithables at both Quarters, David Thomson, David Tyree; James Allen, Michael Sattawhite John Elliss, Maj,^{r} Meriwether's quart,^{rs} John Hambleton & half Sink Quarter, to assist him in Clearing the road he is Overseer of.

April 11, 1721, O.S., p. 44 [new pagination p. 73; Chamberlayne p. 93]
In Obedience to an order of New Kent Court, dated y.ᵉ 14.ᵗʰ day of July 1720 its Ordered that the precincts, whereof Jere; Parker is Surveyor, be divided into two precincts, & that Peter Harrilson be Surveyor of the Lower prec,ᵗ beginning at Ash Cake Road, thence up the road to Magirts path, and that he have Mich,ˡ Gowing's Male Tithables, M,ʳˢ Mary Anderson's Tithables at the Quarter adjoining to that, Geo: Butlers, Henry Tyler's, and his own Tithables to Assist him in the Clearing and keeping that road in good order.

November 6, 1722, O.S., p. 47 [new pagination p. 77 ½; Chamberlayne p. 101]
Order'd, that there be taken out of Tho,ˢ Stanley's gang to assist Andrew Spradling in his precinct, M,ʳ David Crawford, W:ᵐ Cape James Martin, John Mallory, Edw,ᵈ Selby, & Jnᵒ Lewis, with all their Male Tithables

November 6, 1722, O.S., p. 47 [new pagination p. 77 ¾; Chamberlayne p. 101]
In Obedience to an order of court, dated the 2ᵈ of march, 1721, its order'd, that Samuel Knuckols clear a road, from. the upper end of Mattlock's road, to the upper Inhabitants, on the north Side of the South river, and that he have to Assist him, M,ʳ Tho:ˢ Johnson's, M,ʳ David Meriwether's upper Quarter, Jnᵒ Bunch on Taylors Creek, Isaac Johnson, Jnᵒ Bostick, M,ʳ Rich,ᵈ Phillips, with all their Male Tithables.

November 6, 1722, O.S., p. 47 [new pagination p. 77 ¾; Chamberlayne p. 101]
Order'd that there be added to Peter Haroldson's Gang, Alex:ʳ Kersey, Paul Bunch's Quarter, & Luke Anthony.

November 6, 1722, O.S., p. 47 [new pagination p. 77 ¾; Chamberlayne p. 101]
Order'd that Geo: Vaughn, have out of Jeremiah Parkers Gang to assist him, in the road he is Surveyor of, Cornel,ˢ Tinsley, John Cook, Martin Baker, M,ʳ Cha:ˢ Lewis's Quarter, M,ʳ Anthony Waddy's Quarter, & Benj:ᵃ Alsop, and out of Matth,ʷ Jennings's Gang, Cornelius Dabney, Jnᵒ Blalack, Rich,ᵈ Blalack David Lewis, & Jnᵒ Cawley, with all their Male Tithables.

April 16, 1723, O.S., p. 48 [new pagination p. 78; Chamberlayne p. 102]
In Obedience to an Order of Court, dated y,ᵉ 1,ˢᵗ day of Feb,ʳʸ 1723, Appointing John Tinsley to be Surveyor of a Road, to be clear'd from Crumps Creek, by Rich:ᵈ Corleys, to the road by Edw:ᵈ Chambers Sen,ʳ and that he have to assist him, Geo: Davis, Edw:ᵈ Chambers Sen,ʳ James Hooper, Col,ᵒ Birds Middle Quarter, with all their male Tithables to Assist him, to Clear & maintain the said road.

April 28, 1724, O.S., p. 49 [new pagination p. 80; Chamberlayne p. 107]
In obedience to an order of Court dated y.ᵉ 2.ᵈ of June 1721. appointing Jnᵒ English Surveyor of a Road from Stagg Creek to Stony run, bridge, its Orderd, that he have to assist him in Clearing, and maintaining the said road, Jonathan Ashur, Adam Retherford, Cornelius Dabney's Quarter, Cap.ᵗ Hudson's Quarter, John Suttons Quarter, with all their Male Tithables.

April 28, 1724, O.S., p. 49 [new pagination p. 81; Chamberlayne p. 108]
In obedience to an order of Court dated y,ᵉ 3ᵈ of April 1724. Ordering the road that runs by Possom Point, be added to Henry Walkers precinct, Ordered, that he have to assist him, to maintain the said Road, Cap.ᵗ Hudsons home Gang, Jnᵒ Bow, & William Austin.

April 28, 1724, O.S., p. 49 [new pagination p. 81; Chamberlayne p. 108]
In obedience to an order of Court dated y:ᵉ 4.ᵗʰ of 8.ᵇʳ 1723. Ordering Charles Moorman to Succeed Jere: Parker, deceas'd, in yᵉ road he was Surveyor of: Order'd that he have to assist him in maintaining the said road, William Webb, Thomas Johnson, Rich,ᵈ Allen, John Killcrease, Franc,ˢ Clark, John Smithin Tho,ˢ Rowland, William Thacker, John Raglan, Stephen Raglan, Timothy Sullivan, Timothy Reach, & W,ᵐ Harris, with all their male Tithables.

June 12, 1724, O.S., p. 50 [new pagination p. 82; Chamberlayne p. 111]
In Obedience to an order of Court dated y:ᵉ 1.ˢᵗ of November 1723, Jnᵒ Bowles to be Surveyor in making a Road, from Licking hole Swamp, over the lower way of Stony run, so up the said Bowles path to Ash Cake road. it is Orderd, that he have to assist him in Clearing & maintaining that road, Tho:ˢ Harlow, Jnᵒ Harlow, and all the male Tithables on the South Side of Ash Cake road, to Stony run mouth Thence up the Swamp to Harlows

June 12, 1724, O.S., p. 50 [new pagination p. 82; Chamberlayne p. 111]
In Obedience to an order of Court dated y:ᵉ 4.ᵗʰ of 8.ᵇʳ 1723. Ordering Jnᵒ Jones to be Overseer of a road, from the Flax field to M,ʳ Winstons Mill, Orderd, that he have to Assist him in Clearing and maintaining the said road: Col.ᵒ Bird's 2 Quarters Jo: Gentry, M,ʳ Hunt's Quarter: & W,ᵐ Archer, with all their male Tithables.

April 8, 1729, O.S., p. 53 [new pagination p. 89; Chamberlayne p. 121]
Orderd, that Eliezer Davis and his Male Tithables, W,ᵐ Pain and his Male Tithables, Samuel Davis and his Male Tithables, work upon the road whereof John Dabney is Surveyor.

June 16, 1729, O.S., p. 54 [new pagination p. 90; Chamberlayne p. 122]
Orderc'd, that Sam,ˡ Hill and his male Tithables, John Robinson, and his male Tithables, and Simon Wootten, Work upon the road, whereof Col,ᵒ David Meriwether is Surveyor

June 16, 1729, O.S., p. 54 [new pagination p. 90; Chamberlayne p. 122]
Order'd, that W,ᵐ Knuckols work upon y:ᵉ road, whereof John Jones is Surveyor

July 19, 1729, O.S., p. 54 [new pagination p. 91; Chamberlayne p. 123]
Order'd, that John Guess, Alex,ʳ Kersey, Joseph Sperrin, and their male Tithables, work on the road, whereof Peter Harrilson is Surveyor

June 15, 1730, O.S., p. 55 [new pagination p. 92; Chamberlayne p. 126]
Ordered that William Tate have the Tithables of the Rev.ᵈ Zach: Brook and the Tithables of M.ʳ James Whitlock, and the Tithables of James Rice added, to assist him in Clearing the Road whereof he is Surveyor

September 16, 1730, O.S., p. 56 [new pagination p. 94; Chamberlayne p. 128]
Order'd that Rob,ᵗ Tate have the Tithables of George Ross, Henry Kerby, Thomas Reynolds, Joseph Martin, William Melton, John Melton, John Cobbs John Kersey, to assist him in clearing the road whereof he is Surveyor.

September 16, 1730, O.S., p. 56 [new pagination p. 94; Chamberlayne p. 129]
Ordered that John Wooddy have the Tithables of Cap,ᵗ William Macon living at the old Quarter, and Swamp Quarter, Cap,ᵗ Thomas Massie's Tithables at his quarter and Thomas Railey's Tithables, to assist him in Clearing the road, whereof he is Surveyor

September 16, 1730, O.S., p. 56 [new pagination p. 94; Chamberlayne p. 129]
Ordered that the Tithes of the Rev,ᵈ Zach: Brook, James Rice, & M,ʳ James Whitlock and David Tyree, assist James Allen in Clearing the road, whereof he is Surveyor

September 16, 1730, O.S., p. 56 [new pagination p. 94; Chamberlayne p. 129]
Ordered that Sam,ˡ Hill & his Tithes assist Cap,ᵗ William Fleming in Clearing the road whereof he is Surveyor.

September 16, 1730, O.S., p. 56 [new pagination p. 94; Chamberlayne p. 129]
Order'd, that the Tiths of Cap,ᵗ Tho;ˢ Anderson assist Roger Williams in clearing the road whereof he is Surveyor.

May 15, 1731, O.S., p. 56 [new pagination p. 95; Chamberlayne p. 130]
Order'd, that Peter Harralson have two of M,ʳ Prossers Tithables to help Clear the road, whereof he is Surveyor

October 4, 1732, O.S., p. 57 [new pagination p. 97; Chamberlayne p. 134]
Orderd, that Benj;ᵃ Hawkins work on the road, where m,ʳ Bowles is Surveyor and that John Glens Tithes work on the road where m,ʳ Holland is Surveyor

October 4, 1732, O.S., p. 57 [new pagination p. 97; Chamberlayne p. 134]
Orderd, that Ambrose Hundly have John Tinsley, W,ᵐ Clark, Joseph Row, Tho,ˢ Tinsley's Tithes, widow Chambers's Tithes, Edward Chambers Tithes James Hooper & John Rea to assist him in clearing the road whereof he is Surveyor

April 11, 1732, O.S., p. 58 [new pagination p. 98; Chamberlayne p. 134]
Order'd that the Tithables of Charles Hudson Gent, Cornelius Dabney, Cornel,ˢ Tinsley, W,ᵐ Harris, Matthew Pate, David Hains, John Mitchel & John Rowland, assist John Ragland to Clear the road whereof he is Appointed Surveyor

April 11, 1732, O.S., p. 58 [new pagination p. 98; Chamberlayne p. 134]
Orderd that the Tithables of Henry Tyler, Nich,ᵒ Madelin, Joseph Gentry Sarah Archer, and W,ᵐ Gentry (if he be willing,) be added to Peter Harralsons gang, to assist him in Clearing his road

April 11, 1732, O.S., p. 58 [new pagination p. 98; Chamberlayne p. 135]
Order'd, that John Guess be added to John Hudson's gang,

April 11, 1732, O.S., p. 58 [new pagination p. 98; Chamberlayne p. 135]
Order'd that Anthony Pouncy and his Tithables be added to Ralph Hunt's gang

June 2, 1733, O.S., p. 58 [new pagination p. 99; Chamberlayne p. 135]
Orderd that Rich:ᵈ Corley have W;ᵐ Chambers and his Tithes, John Tinsley & his Tithes, John Browning and his Tithes, and all his own sons to assist him Clearing the Road, whereof he is Surveyor.

June 2, 1733, O.S., p. 58 [new pagination p. 99; Chamberlayne p. 136]
Ordered, that Paul Harralson have Rob,ᵗ Francis, John Simmons and one of Col,ᵒ Birds Tithes to assist him in Clearing his road

[torn] 19, 1734, O.S., p. 60 [new pagination p. 102; Chamberlayne p. 140]
Order'd, that M,ʳ Thomas Johnson have the following Tithables to help Clear his road, Charles Johnson, M,ʳ Hollands Titheables, at black Haw William Allens Tithables, Robᵗ Allens Tithables, Joseph Thompsons Tithables Benj,ᵃ Bowles Tithables, John Harlows Tithables, Tho,ˢ Harlows Tithables Charles Andersons Tithables, John Williamson's Tithables

[torn] 19, 1734, O.S., p. 60 [new pagination p. 102; Chamberlayne p. 140]
Order'd, that Richard Winn have Rob,ᵗ Allen's Tithables, Cha,ˢ Talley's William Nichols, Tho,ˢ Johnson's and Abraham Bakers Tithables to assist him in Clearing his road.

[torn] 19, 1734, O.S., p. 60 [new pagination p. 102; Chamberlayne p. 141]
Orderd, that Tho:ˢ Saterwhite have David Lyles Tithes Nathaniel Baughons, Tho,ˢ Moselys; W,ᵐ Baughon's, W,ᵐ Hughs's James Piron Jun,ʳ, Jnᵒ Piron John Ellis Michael Saterwhite, Charles Piron and James Piron, Senʳ tithables to assist him in Clearing the road, whereof he is Surveyor.

[torn] 19, 1734, O.S., p. 60 [new pagination p. 103; Chamberlayne p. 141]
Orderd, that Benj,ᵃ Johnson, have the Tithables of John Price, Tho,ˢ Grant; Edw:ᵈ Harris, David Alvis, Tho,ˢ Winpenney, W,ᵐ Hix, Wᵐ Cawthon, Nich,ᵒ Gentry, Jnᵒ Ross, and Laurence Forguson to assist him in Clearing the road whereof he is Surveyor

[torn] 19, 1734, O.S., p. 60 [new pagination p. 103; Chamberlayne p. 141]
Peter Marks Tithables are added to John Wingfields road

October 18, 1735, O.S., p. 61 [new pagination p. 104; Chamberlayne p. 143]
Ordered that Sam;ˡ Gentry have the Tithables of Sam,ˡ Pryor, Nich,ᵒ Gentry James M,ᶜcloughland; W,ᵐ M,ᶜgillary, George Lovel, John Lovel, & Wᵐ Cawthon, to Assist him in Clearing the road, whereof he is Surveyor

October 18, 1735, O.S., p. 61 [new pagination p. 104; Chamberlayne p. 144]
Orderd that there be added to George Jones's Gang, Tho:^{s} Stanley; Ja,^{s} Blackwell Matthew Turner, and Rob,^{t} Glass's Tithables

October 18, 1735, O.S., p. 61 [new pagination p. 105; Chamberlayne p. 144]
Orderd that there be added to Edw,^{d} Sims gang, W,^{m} Gentry, Alex,^{r} Kersey, and Nich,^{o} Needin

October 15, 1737, O.S., p. 63 [new pagination p. 109; Chamberlayne p. 150]
Ordered that George Davis have the Tithables of W,^{m} Thacker, John Rowland, Edw:^{d} England, Jacob King, and Robert Wade, to help Clear the road whereof he is Surveyor.

November 15, 1737, O.S., p. 64 [new pagination p. 110; Chamberlayne p. 152]
Orderd, that John Jones's Tithables do maintain the new road, to be cleard from the new Glebe of this parish, into y:^{e} road that leads to y:^{e} lower Church of which John Tinsley Sen,^{r} is Overseer

November 15, 1737, O.S., p. 64 [new pagination p. 110; Chamberlayne p. 152]
Ordere'd, that Nicholas Mills Jun,^{r} & his Tithables, James Wade, Rob,^{t} Whealer, John Humber be added to the Gang, of which Col,^{o} David Meriwether is overseer

May 29, 1739, O.S., p. 65 [new pagination p. 113; Chamberlayne p. 157]
Ordered that William Winston have M,^{rs} Anderson's People, James Wade's, Nicholas Mill's assign'd him to clear the road over Mahixon Mill, of which he is Overseer

September 11, 1739, O.S., p. 66 [new pagination p. 114; Chamberlayne p. 158]
Ordered, that Edw:^{d} England and Robert Wade's people, & Timothy Williams be taken out of John Glenn's Gang, and added to Jacob Kings Company, on the Road he is Surveyor of.

October 8, 1743, O.S., p. 71 [new pagination p. 124; Chamberlayne p. 176]
Order'd that Joseph Gentry Sen,^{r} and Jacob Hundley be added to John Jones's Gang, to Clear the road from the Glebe House Downwards

[Last road-related order in the vestry book]

APPENDIX

PROCESSIONING AND TOBACCO VIEWING ORDERS
WITH REFERENCES TO ROADS

NOTE: Among their other responsibilities, the vestry was involved in identifying districts, or "precincts," for processioning (periodic identification of property boundaries) and tobacco viewing, or "telling" (inspection of tobacco fields to ensure that suckers [the secondary, inferior shoots] were not being cultivated). The Parish was divided into 39 precincts for land processioning. The following entries are not road orders but rather are processioning or tobacco viewing orders that make reference to roads.

June 12, 1724, O.S., p. 50 [new pagination p. 82; Chamberlayne p. 109]

To begin at y:ᵉ mouth of Tottopottomoys Creek, so up yᵉ River to Crumps creek so up y:ᵉ south side of the said Creek to precimmon Ford road; thence along y:ᵉ said road to Tottopottomoys Creek, then down the said Creek to y:ᵉ river. & that M,ʳ Ralph Crutchfield and M,ʳ John Talley be Tellers of it.

June 12, 1724, O.S., p. 50 [new pagination p. 82; Chamberlayne p. 110]

To begin at the mouth of Crumps Creek, so up the river to Machumps Creek, then up the said Creek to the head, Benj,ᵃ Alsup the highest, thence to Cross to the head of Tottopottomoy's Creek, thence down to Precimmon Ford road, then along the said road to the head of Crumps Creek then down y:ᵉ said creek to the river. & that M,ʳ Jnᵒ Bowles & M,ʳ Hen: Walker be tellers of it.

June 12, 1724, O.S., p. 50 [new pagination p. 82; Chamberlayne p. 110]

To begin at y:ᵉ mouth of Machumps Creek, so up the river to the mouth of Stagg creek, thence to the head of the said Creek, from thence to the head of Grassey Swamp, so down yᵉ said Swamp to Chickahominy Swamp, then down the said Swamp to M,ʳ Macon's Quarter, from thence to Precimmon Ford road, then along the said road to Tottopottomoy's Creek, then up the said Creek to the head, thence a Cross to Benj,ᵃ Alsup's, then down Machumps Creek to the river, & y,ᵗ M,ʳ Jnᵒ Richardson; & M,ʳ David Gwinn be the Tellers of it

June 16, 1729, O.S., p. 54 [new pagination p. 90; Chamberlayne p. 122]

Ordered that all the Tobacco Tellers in this parish be continued in the respective precincts where they told last year; only the precincts where David Lewis, and Ralph Hunt told last year is bounded from Benj,ᵃ Alsop's to Francis Clark's on Stony run, so down that run to Chickahomony Swamp, then down the Swamp to Precimmon ford road, Only Omitting Capᵗ Massey's Quarter on the mouth of Stony run

Nov. 30, 1763, N.S., no original pagination visible [new pagination p. 308; Chamberlayne pp. 416-417]

[Boundaries of Processioning Precinct No. 6] . . . Lands of James Cawthon, James Crenshaw, John Spraddling, Nicholas Gentry, Samuel Pryor, W;^m Berry's Orphans, William Cawthon, James Philips, William Harris, and that James Mitchell and William Morrice do see the said processioning performed, and return the proceedings according to Law

Pursuant to the Above Order, M,^r Mitchel being Absent, the Subscriber hath Seen the Lands above mention'd, procession'd, betwixt Beever Creek, and the River, to Ash Cake Road; which includes Other Lands, not Mentioned in the Order.

William Morris

November 30, 1763, N.S., no original pagination visible [new pagination p. 316; Chamberlayne p. 428]

[Boundaries of Processioning Precinct No. 22] . . .the lands of John White, Tho,^s Easts orphans Kelly Hughes Thomas Wild, John Forsie, James Allen Turner Richardson Philip Frazier, Anthony Winston, William Hughes, and that James Allen and Turner Richardson see the processioning perform'd, and return their proceedings according to law. . .

In Obedience to the within Order we the subscribers has seen the Lines of all the land peacably procession'd, from the Road crossing Chickahomeny at the three Runs Bridge, down said Swamp, to Beaver dam Swomp, which includes the lands of Samuel Morris, William Hughs, William Craghead, John Ellis's orphans, Aaron Trueheart, Thomas Wild, Robt Smith, Rob,^t Lee, Barrot White, Anthony Winston Gent. Matthew Whitlock, Charles Richardson John Richardson Elizabeth Tyree, Philip Frazier, the Subscribers examined a Line between Aaron Trueheart & William Hughes, which we have returned to the Wardens according to Law

James Allen
Turner Richardson

INDEX

This index is arranged by subject: Bridges; Church, Glebes, Parishes; County Government; Fords; Land Features; Mills; Miscellaneous Subjects (houses, landmarks, neighborhoods, plantations, quarters, stores, etc.); Personal Names; Rivers, Runs, Swamps and other Water Features; Roads.

Edward Clark's, 1
Francis Clark's on Stony run, 13
Alexr. Cock's, 7
Richd. Corley's, 8
lands of William Craghead, 14
lands of James Crenshaw, 14
Cornelius Dabney's quarter, 8
Mr. Geo. Dabney's quarter, 6
Col. Duke's quarter, 5
lands of Thos. East's orphans, 14
lands of John Ellis's orphans, 14
the Flax field, 9
lands of John Forsie, 14
lands of Philip Frazier, 14
lands of Nicholas Gentry, 14
Half Sink/Half Sink quarter, 5, 7
Harding's Landing (formerly Youels, on
        Pamunkey River), 4, 5, 6
Harding's store house, 6
Harlow's, 9
lands of William Harris, 14
Mr. Holland's tithables/property, at
        Black Haw, 11
Capt. Hudson's quarter, 8
lands of Kelly Hughes, 14
lands of William Hughes/Hughs, 14
Line between William Hughes and
        Aaron Trueheart, 14
Mr. Hunt's quarter, 9
Place where _____ Lancaster formerly
        dwelt, 3
Nicholas Lawson's plantation (in St.
        Peter's parish), 1
lands of Robt. Lee, 14
Mr. Chas. Lewis's quarter, 8
Mr. Macon's quarter, 13
Capt. William Macon's old quarter, 10
Capt. William Macon's Swamp quarter,
        10
Mahixon, 3
Capt. Massey's quarter on the mouth of
        Stony run, 13
Capt. Thomas Massie's quarter, 10
Maj. Meriwether's lower quarter, 5
Maj. Meriwether's quarters, 7
Mr. David Meriwether's upper quarter, 8

Maj. Nicho. Meriwether's, 7
The Middle quarter, 3
Edward Moor's, 1
lands of Samuel Morris, 14
the Pipeing Tree (on Pamunkey River),
        4, 5, 6
Harding's Landing (formerly Youels, on
        Pamunkey River), 4, 5, 6
Youels Landing (later Harding's, on
        Pamunkey River), 4
Clearing Paumounkey (Pamunkey)
        River (from the Pipeing Tree to
        Harding's [formerly Youels]
        Landing), 4, 5, 6
lands of James Philips, 14
the Pipeing Tree (on Pamunkey River),
        4, 5, 6
Polegreen's quarter, 3
Polegreen's old field, 5, 6
lands of Samuel Pryor, 14
lands of Charles Richardson, 14
lands of John Richardson, 14
lands of Turner Richardson, 14
John Sandidge's plantation, 1
lands of Robt. Smith, 14
lands of John Spraddling, 14
John Suttons quarter, 8
the old schoolhouse near Samuel
        Waddy's plantation, 5
Mr. (Roger) Thomsons home house, 6
Cornelius Tinsley's, 7
lands of Aaron Trueheart, 14
Line between Aaron Trueheart &
        William Hughes, 14
George Turner's, 1
lands of Elizabeth Tyree, 14
the Upper Inhabitants, 8
Mr. Anthony Waddy's quarter, 8
Samuel Waddy's/Samuel Waddy's
        plantation, 5, 7
lands of Barrot White, 14
lands of John White, 14
lands of Thomas Wild, 14
lands of Anthony Winston Gent., 14
lands of Matthew Whitlock, 14

Youels Landing (later Harding's, on Pamunkey River), 4

Personal Names

[torn]eadly, Jno, 3
[torn-An?]nderson, 3
Allen, James, 7, 10, 14
Allen, Rennold, 5
Allen, Richd., 6, 9
Allen, Robt., 11(2)
Allen, William, 11
Alsop, Benja., 8, 13
Alsup, Benja., 13(2)
Alvis, David, 11
Anderson, Charles, 11
Anderson, Cicilia, 7
Anderson, Mr. David, 4, 5, 6
Anderson, Mr. John/Jno. 7(2)
Anderson, Mrs. Mary, 7, 8
Anderson, Mrs., 12
Anderson, Capt. Robert, 4
Anderson, Thos./Capt. Thos., 7, 10
Anthony, Luke, 8
Anthony, Mark, 4
Archer, Sarah, 10
Archer, Wm., 9
Ashur, Jonathan, 8
Austin, William, 9
Bailey, Thos., 4
Baker, Abraham, 11
Baker, Martin, 8
Basset, Thos., 5
Bassett, Col.., 5
Baughan, John Sr., 1
Baughon, Joseph, 4
Baughon, Nathaniel, 11
Baughon, Wm., 11
Berry, Wm.'s orphans, 14
Bird, Col., 8, 9, 11
Blackwell, Jas., 12
Blalack, Jno., 8
Blalack, Richd., 8
Bostick, Cha., 6
Bostick, Jno., 8

Bow, Henry, 7
Bow, Jno., 9
Bowe, Henry, 4, 6
Bowle, Thos., 5
Bowles, Benja., 11
Bowles, Jno./Mr. Jno., 9, 13
Bowles, Mr., 10
Bowls, Thomas, 4
Brabant, Doctor, 3
Brook, Rev. Zach., 9, 10
Brown, Joseph, 5
Browning, John, 11
Bullock, Edward, 4
Bunch, Jno., 8
Bunch, Paul, 6, 8
Burnett, Elizabeth, 4
Butler, Geo., 8
Byas, John, 5
Cacy, 4
Caisey, Thos., 4
Cape, Wm., 8
Cawley, Jno., 8
Cawthon, James, 14
Cawthon, William/Wm., 11(2), 14
Chambers, Edward, 5, 10
Chambers, Edwd. Sr., 8
Chambers, Widow, 10
Chambers, Wm., 11
Chiles, Mr. Henry, 5(2), 6
Clark, Christopher/ Xphr., 4, 5
Clark, Edward/ Edwd., 1, 4, 5
Clark, Frances/Francis/Francs., 6, 9, 13
Clark, Wm., 10
Clough, Md., 5
Cobbs, John, 10
Cock, Alexander/Alexr./Mr. Alexr., 4, 6, 7
Cook, Abraham, 4, 5
Cook, John, 8
Cook, Robt., 4
Corley, Jno., 6
Corley, Richd., 8, 11
Corley, Richard Jr., 5
Corley, Richard's (?) sons, 11
Crafford, Mr., 4
Craghead, William, 14

Crawford, Mr. David, 8
Crenshaw, James, 14
Crutchfield, Mr. Ralph, 13
Dabney, Cornelius, 8(2), 10
Dabney, Mr. Geo., 6
Dabney, John, 9
Davis, Eliezer, 9
Davis, Ely, 3
Davis, George/Geo., 8, 12
Davis, Samuel, 9
Dick, Thos., 6
Dishman, Daniel, 5
Duke, Col., 5
East, Thos., 5
East, Thos.'s orphans, 14
Elderkin, John, 3
Ellis, John, 11
Ellis, John's orphans, 14
Elliss, John, 7
England, Edwd., 12(2)
English, Jno., 6, 8
Esther, Frances, 4
Evins, Elizabeth, 4
Farmur, Henry, 5
Fleming, Capt. William, 10
Flemming, Mr. Wm., 7(2)
Forguson, Laurence, 11
Forsie, John, 14
Francis, Robt., 11
Frazier, Philip, 14(2)
Freeman, Wm., 4
Gentry, Jo., 9
Gentry, Joseph, 5, 10
Gentry, Joseph Sr., 12
Gentry, Nicholas/Nicho./Nichs., 5(2),
    11(2), 14
Gentry, Saml., 6, 11
Gentry, Wm., 10, 12
Gibson, Gilbert, 6, 7
Glass, Robt., 12
Glass, Thomas, 7
Glen, John, 10
Glenn, John/Mr. John, 5, 6, 7, 12
Gowing, Michl., 8
Grant, Thos., 11
Guess, John, 9, 11

Guntin, John, 5
Gwinn, Mr. David, 13
Hains, David, 10
Hall, John, 4
Hambleton, John, 7(2)
Hambleton, Joseph, 5
Harding, 4, 5, 6(2),
Harlow, John/Jno., 9, 11
Harlow, Thos., 9, 11
Haroldson, Peter, 8
Harralson, Paul, 11
Harralson, Peter, 10(2)
Harrilson, Peter, 8, 9
Harris, Edwd., 3, 11
Harris, John, 5
Harris, Thomas, 6
Harris, William/Wm., 9, 10, 14
Harriss, William, 4
Hart, John, 6
Hatfield, Wm., 5
Hawkins, Benja., 10
Hill, Jno., 7
Hill, Saml., 9, 10
Hix, Wm., 11
Hodgkinson, Nathl., 5
Hodkison, Nathaniel, 4
Hogg, William/Wm., 4, 5
Holland, Mr., 10, 11
Hooper, James, 8, 10
Horsley, Mr. Rowland, 4
Howlet, William, 5
Hudson, Capt., 8, 9
Hudson, Charles Gent./Mr. Cha., 7, 10
Hudson, John, 6, 11
Hughes, Kelly, 14
Hughes, William, 14(2)
Hughs, William/Wm., 11, 14
Humber, John, 12
Hundley, Jacob, 12
Hundly, Ambrose, 10
Hunt, Mr., 9
Hunt, Ralph, 11, 13
Jennings, James, 3
Jennings, Matthw., 8
Johnson, Benja., 11
Johnson, Charles, 11

Johnson, Isaac, 8
Johnson, Thomas/Thos./Mr. Thos., 4,
    8, 9, 11(2)
Johnston, John, 4
Jones, George, 12
Jones, John/Jno., 9(2), 12(2)
Kerby, Henry, 10
Kersey, Alexr., 8, 9, 12
Kersey, John, 10
Kersey, Thos., 5
Killcrease, John, 9
Kimbrow, John Jr., 4, 5
King, Jacob, 12(2)
Knuckols, Samuel, 8
Knuckols, Wm., 9
Lancaster, _____, 3
Lawson, John, 4
Lawson, Nicholas, 1
Lee, Robt., 14
Lewis, 8
Lewis, Mr. Chas., 8
Lewis, David, 13
Lewis, Esquire, 5
Lewis, Jno./Mr. John, 1, 8
Lewis, John Jr., 7
Lovel, George, 11
Lovel, John, 11
Lyle, David, 11
Macon, Capt. William, 10
Macon, Mr. Jno., 7
Macon, Mr., 13
Madelin, Nicho., 10
Magirt, 8
Mallory, John, 8
Mark, Peter, 11
Martin, James, 8
Martin, Joseph, 10
Mask, Mr. John, 5
Massey, Capt., 13
Massie, Capt. Thomas, 10
Mattlock, 8
Mccloughland, James, 11
Mcgillary, Wm., 11
Mckenny, Alexander, 4
Mckensie, Alexr., 5
Megirt, 7

Melton, John, 10
Melton, William, 10
Meriwether, Col. David/Mr. David, 7(2),
    8, 9, 12
Meriwether, Maj., 4, 5, 7
Meriwether, Maj. Nicho., 7
Mills, Henry, 5
Mills, Nicholas Jr., 12
Mills, Nicholas, 12
Mills, Robt., 6
Mitchel, John, 10
Mitchell, James, 14
Moor, Edward, 1
Moorman, Charles, 9
Morrice, William, 14
Morris, Samuel, 14
Morris, William, 14
Mosely, Thos., 11
Needin, Nicho., 12
Netherland, Robt., 7
Nichols, William, 11
Nuckols, James, 5
Pain, Wm., 9
Parker, Jere./Jeremiah, 4, 6, 7, 8(2)
Parker, Jere. (deceased), 9
Parrish, Humphrey, 4
Pate, Matthew, 10
Peak, Thomas, 4
Penix, Edward, 7
Perkins, John Jr., 5
Perkins, John Sr., 5
Philips, George, 7
Philips, James, 14
Phillips, Mr. Richd., 8
Pirant, Jno., 5
Piron, Charles, 11
Piron, James Jr., 11
Piron, James Sr., 11
Piron, Jno., 11
Poind[torn -exter?], Mr. Thomas, 3
Polegreen, 5
Polesgreen, 6
Poors, Joseph, 5
Pouncy, Anthony, 11
Price, John, 11
Prosser, Mr., 10

Pryor, Samuel/Saml., 11, 14
Raglan, John, 9
Raglan, Stephen, 9
Ragland, John, 10
Raglin, Stephen, 6
Railey, Thomas, 10
Ray, John/[torn]hn, 3, 6
Rea, John, 10
Reach, Timothy, 9
Rennolds, Samuel, 5
Retherford, Adam, 8
Reynolds, Thomas, 10
Rhodes, Charles, 5
Rice, James, 9, 10
Richardson, Charles, 14
Richardson, John/Mr. Jno., 13, 14
Richardson, Turner, 14
Robinson, John, 9
Ross, George, 10
Ross, Jno., 11
Row, Joseph, 10
Rowland, John, 10, 12
Rowland, Thos., 9
Sandidge, John, 1
Saterwhite, Michael, 11
Saterwhite, Thos., 11
Sattawhite, Michael, 7
Sattawhite, Thos., 7
Saunders, Jno., 7
Selby, Edwd., 8
Sentre, Stephen, 4
Sheperson, Geo., 3
Simmons, John, 11
Sims, Edwd., 12
Smith, Robt., 14
Smith, Roger, 5
Smithin, John, 9
Sperrin, Joseph, 9
Sperring, Saml., 6
Spraddling, John, 14
Spradling, Andrew, 8
Stanley, Thomas/Thos., 7, 8
Stanley, Thos., 12
Sullivan, Timothy, 9
Sutton, John, 8
Talley, Chas., 11

Talley, Mr. John, 13
Talley, William, 7
Tap, Jno., 3
Tate, James, 7
Tate, Robt., 10
Tate, William, 9
Terrell, William, 4
Thacker, William/Wm., 6, 9, 12
Thomas, Geo., 7
Thompson, Joseph, 11
Thomson, David, 7(2)
Thomson, Capt. Roger/Roger Gent., 5, 6
Tickle, Mr. Peter, 5
Tinsley, Cornelius/Cornels., 7, 8, 10
Tinsley, John, 5, 8, 10, 11
Tinsley, John Sr., 12
Tinsley, Thos., 10
Trueheart, Aaron, 14
Turner, George, 1
Turner, Matthew, 12
Tyler, Henry, 8, 10
Tyler, John, 5
Tyree, David, 7, 10
Tyree, Elizabeth, 14
Vaughn, Geo., 8
Venable, John/Jno., 4, 6
Waddy, Mr. Anthony, 8
Waddy, Samuel, 4, 5(2), 7
Wade, James, 12
Wade, Robert, 12(2)
Walker, Henry/Mr. Hen., 9, 13
Walker, Robt., 5
Webb, William/Wm., 6, 9
Wetherford, Thos., 4, 6
Wetherford, William, 4
Whealer, Robt., 12
White, Barrot, 14
White, John/Mr. John/Mr. Jno., 3, 4,
    5(2), 14
Whitlock, Matthew, 14
Whitlock, Mr. James, 9, 10
Wild, Thomas, 14(2)
Williams, Roger, 10
Williams, Timothy, 12
Williams, William, 4
Williamson, John, 11

Wingfield, John, 11
Winn, Richard, 11
Winpenney, Thos., 11
Winston, Anthony (and Gent.), 14(2)
Winston, Isaac/ Issack, 4, 5
Winston, Mr., 9
Winston, William, 12
Wooddy, John, 10
Wootten, Simon, 9
Wootton, John, 4
Youel, 4
Youell, Widow 3

Rivers, Runs, Swamps and other Water Features

_____y's Swamp, 3
Bassets runs, 6
Beaver Dam/Bever Dam Swamp, 3, 4, 14
Beever Creek, 14
Ceder Creek, 7
Chickahomeny/Chickahomony/ Chickohommany Swamp, 1, 4, 7, 13(2), 14
the three runs of Chickohommany Swamp, 4, 14

Crumps creek, 5, 8, 13(2)
Deep Swamp, 5
Elder Swamp, 3
The South River in the Forks, 4
Golden Mine Creek, 6
Grassey Swamp, 13
Licking hole Swamp, 9
Little Creek (branch of Mattedicun), 3
Machumps Creek, 7, 13(2)
Maccadecum creek, 1
branch of Mattedicun (Little Creek), 3
the fork (of Mattedicun?), 3
the main Swamp, 3
Newfound River, 7
Paumounkey/Paumonkey River, 4, 5(2)
the River, 13(3), 14
South River, 8
The South River in the Forks, 4
Stagg Creek, 8, 13
Stone Horse Creek, 6
Stony Run, 6(2), 7, 8, 9, 13
Stony Swamp, 4
Taylors Creek, 8
the three runs of Chickohommany Swamp, 4, 14
Tottopottomoys Creek, 3(2), 7(2), 13(2)

Roads

Roads are cross-indexed to all locations and persons mentioned. Descriptions have been standardized to aid in identifying roads and to simplify the preparation of this index. This was a necessity since many road descriptions changed slightly as different landmarks were cited. Various roads went under similar general descriptions and the reader should bear this in mind when determining the identity of each road.

Bridle Road from John Anderson's to Alexr. Cocks, 7

Ash Cake Road, 14

Ash Cake Road to Magirts [see also Megirt] path, 8

Road from Licking hole Swamp, crossing Stony run, and up John Bowles path to Ash Cake road, 9

Road from Possom Point into the main road, leading down the country, below Bassets runs, 6

the Queens high road to the rolling road leading from Edward Moor's to George Turner's and the plantation of John Baughan Sr., 1

Road from Licking hole Swamp, crossing Stony run, and up John Bowles path to Ash Cake road, 9

New road from Cacy's old field, along an old path to Stony Swamp, and another path to Mr. Crafford's mill, 4

Road from Ceder Creek to the road that goes to New Market mill, 7

Road to be cleared from Crumps Creek, by Richd. Corley's, to the road by Edwd. Chambers Sr., 8

Bridle road from Maj. Meriwether's mill to the three runs of Chickahominy Swamp, 4

the Road crossing Chickahominy at the Three Runs bridge, 14

new road, to be cleared from the new glebe of the parish, into the road that leads to the lower Church, 12

Road from Maj. Nicho. Meriwether's to the new Church, 7

Bridle Road from John Anderson's to Alexr. Cocks, 7

Road to be cleared from Crumps Creek, by Richd. Corley's, to the road by Edwd. Chambers Sr., 8

New road from Cacy's old field, along an old path to Stony Swamp, and another path to Mr. Crafford's mill, 4

Road to be cleared from Crumps Creek, by Richd. Corley's, to the road by Edwd. Chambers Sr., 8

Precimmon ford road to the head of Crumps Creek, 13

road from the Flax field to Mr. Winston's mill, 9

road from Mr. Wm. Flemming's mill to Mahixen path, 7

New road in the Forks, 4

new road, to be cleared from the new glebe of the parish, into the road that leads to the lower Church, 12

the road from the Glebe house downwards, 12

Road from Mr. John White's mill, to Half Sink, 5

road from Stony Run downward to Half Sink road, 6

Road from Polegreen's old field, to Harding's store house, 6

Main road from Esquire Lewis's mill, to the old schoolhouse near Samuel Waddy's plantation, 5

Road from Licking hole Swamp, crossing Stony run, and up John Bowles path to Ash Cake road, 9

Ash Cake Road to Magirts [see also Megirt] path, 8

road from Mr. Wm. Flemming's mill to Mahixen path, 7

the road over Mahixon mill, 12

Road from the upper end of Mattlock's road, to the upper Inhabitants, on the north side of the South River, 8

Megirts path [see also Magirt], 7

Bridle road from Maj. Meriwether's mill to the three runs of Chickahominy Swamp, 4

Road from Maj. Nicho. Meriwether's to the new Church, 7

the Queens high road to the rolling road leading from Edward Moor's to George Turner's and the plantation of John Baughan Sr., 1

Road from Ceder Creek to the road that goes to New Market mill, 7

Road from Mr. John White's mill to Polegreen's old field, 5

Road from Polegreen's old field, to Harding's store house, 6

road that runs by Possom Point, 9

Road from Possom Point into the main road, leading down the country, below Bassets runs, 6

Precimmon ford road, 13

Precimmon ford road to Tottopottomoys Creek, 13(2)

Precimmon ford road to the head of Crumps Creek, 13

the Queens high road to the rolling road leading from Edward Moor's to George Turner's and the plantation of John Baughan Sr., 1

Main road from Esquire Lewis's mill, to the old schoolhouse near Samuel Waddy's plantation, 5

Road from the upper end of Mattlock's road, to the upper Inhabitants, on the north side of the South River, 8

Road from Stagg Creek to Stony Run bridge, 8

Road from Stone Horse Creek to Stony Run, 6

Road from Stone Horse Creek to Stony Run, 6

road from Stony Run downward to Half Sink road, 6

Road from Licking hole Swamp, crossing Stony run, and up John Bowles path to Ash Cake road, 9

Road from Stagg Creek to Stony Run bridge, 8

New road from Cacy's old field, along an old path to Stony Swamp, and another path to Mr. Crafford's mill, 4

Bridle Road from Maj. Meriwether's mill to the three runs of Chickahominy Swamp, 4

the road crossing Chickahominy at the Three Runs bridge, 14

road from Tottopottomoys Creek to Samuel Waddy's, 7

Precimmon ford road to Tottopottomoys Creek, 13(2)

the Queens high road to the rolling road leading from Edward Moor's to George Turner's and the plantation of John Baughan Sr., 1

Road from the upper end of Mattlock's road, to the upper Inhabitants, on the north side of the South River, 8

Main road from Esquire Lewis's mill, to the old schoolhouse near Samuel Waddy's plantation, 5

road from Tottopottomoys Creek to Samuel Waddy's, 7

Road from Mr. John White's mill, to Half Sink, 5

Road from Mr. John White's mill to Polegreen's old field, 5

road from the Flax field to Mr. Winston's mill, 9

www.ingramcontent.com/pod-product-compliance
Lightning Source LLC
Chambersburg PA
CBHW050906100426
42737CB00048B/3249